Made in the USA
Monee, IL
23 May 2022

96925334R00083